Jan 2017

GAME-CHANGING ATHLETES

ALTHEA GIBSON AND ARTHUR ASHE

Breaking Down Tennis's Color Barrier

Jackie F. Stanmyre

Cavendish
Square

New York

Published in 2016 by Cavendish Square Publishing, LLC
243 5th Avenue, Suite 136, New York, NY 10016

Copyright © 2016 by Cavendish Square Publishing, LLC

First Edition

Website: cavendishsq.com

This publication represents the opinions and views of the author based on his or her personal experience, knowledge, and research. The information in this book serves as a general guide only. The author and publisher have used their best efforts in preparing this book and disclaim liability rising directly or indirectly from the use and application of this book.

CPSIA Compliance Information: Batch #CW16CSQ

All websites were available and accurate when this book was sent to press.

Library of Congress Cataloging-in-Publication Data

Stanmyre, Jackie
Althea Gibson and Arthur Ashe: breaking down tennis's color barrier / Jackie Stanmyre.
pages cm. — (Game-changing athletes)
Includes bibliographical references and index.
ISBN 978-1-5026-1037-9 (hardcover) ISBN 978-1-5026-1055-3 (ebook)
1. Gibson, Althea, 1927-2003—Juvenile literature. 2. African American women tennis players—Biography—Juvenile literature. 3. Ashe, Arthur—Juvenile literature. 4. African American tennis players—Biography—Juvenile literature. 5. Tennis players—United States—Biography—Juvenile literature. I. Title.
GV994.G53S68 2016
796.3420922—dc23
[B]

2015027433

Editorial Director: David McNamara
Editor: Fletcher Doyle
Copy Editor: Rebecca Rohan
Art Director: Jeffrey Talbot
Designer: Joseph Macri
enior Production Manager: Jennifer Ryder-Talbot
Production Editor: Renni Johnson
Photo Research: J8 Media

The photographs in this book are used by permission and through the courtesy of: Norman Potter/Express/Getty Images, front, back cover and throughout the book; CBS via Getty Images, Hulton Archive/Getty Images, front cover; AP Photo, 5, 28, 54; Gordon Parks/The LIFE Picture Collection/Getty Images, 8; File: Althea Gibson/New York World-Telegram and the Sun staff photographer: Fred Palumbo/Library of Congress Prints and Photographs Division/New York World-Telegram and the Sun Newspaper Photograph Collection/http://hdl.loc.gov/loc.pnp/cph.3c14745 NYWTS.jpg /Wikimedia Commons, 11; AP Photo/Elise Amendola, 12; File: Johnson House Lynchburg Nov 08.JPG /Pubdog/Wikimedia Commons, 15; AP Photo/Marty Lederhandler, 18, 74; Top Foto/The Image Works, 24; AFP/Getty Images, 31; Keystone/Getty Images, 34; Reg Speller/Fox Photos/Hulton Archive/Getty Images, 42; Phil Greitzer/NY Daily News Archive via Getty Images, 44-45; AP Photo/Harry Harris, 48, 83; Mike Lien/New York Times Co./Getty Images, 57; Walter Kelleher/NY Daily News Archive via Getty Images, 61; Gerry Cranham/The LIFE Images Collection/Getty Images, 64; Tony Triolo/Sports Illustrated/Getty Images, 68; Focus on Sport/Getty Images, 71; AP Photo/George Wildman, 79; Ron Burton/Keystone/Hulton Archive/Getty Images, 84; John Pedin/NY Daily News via Getty Images, 87; Matthew Stockman/Getty Images, 90; File: Serena and Venus Williams (9630777503).jpg/Edwin Martinez (http://www.flickr.com/people/22705753@N06) from The Bronx/Wikimedia Commons, 93; File: Althea Gibson statue.jpg/Sculpture: Thomas Jay Warren/Image: DoctorJoeE/Wikimedia Commons, 95; Ivan Nikolov/WENN.com/age footstock.com, 98-99.

Printed in the United States of America

CONTENTS

INTRODUCTION

Before the **civil rights movement** had truly begun in the United States, the athletic fields and courts were becoming a frontier for breaking down racial barriers. The discriminatory policies and sentiments that plagued much of the nation, however, created obstacles for leading African-American athletes. This was particularly true in tennis, a sport long known for its elite, rich, and white history.

While many competitions barred African Americans, a few integrated events provided a platform for a handful of athletes to show their worth on the courts. The struggle was long, arduous, and often took a thick skin to navigate. Two such tennis players can be credited for opening doors by combining the courage to take on those who saw them as less-than-equal with the determination to use their athletic gifts to their fullest.

Althea Gibson, a self-proclaimed tomboy, was known in her neighborhood as the toughest competitor, boy or girl, in almost any sport. Her tennis story began after she showed a knack for **paddle tennis**, a court game similar to ping-pong. She gained acclaim from adults who ultimately guided her through her teenage years to

Tennis greats Arthur Ashe (*left*) and Althea Gibson (*right*), who molded future generations of tennis players through their courage to compete, met up-and-coming player Derek Irby in 1976 at a celebrity tournament sponsored by the United Negro College Fund.

opportunities that took her far from her parents' home. They helped her over the hurdle of discrimination set up by naysayers who believed she didn't deserve a place on the courts long occupied only by whites. Gibson didn't fight these battles with her words, but with her tennis racket. She made it impossible for those in the highest ranks to ignore her immense talents. While her journey was anything but smooth, Gibson ultimately made it to the upper echelon of tennis, winning the US Tennis Championships (the predecessor to the US Open) and Wimbledon, among many other titles. Gibson was not an activist in the traditional sense, and rarely did she speak up about equal rights, but through her athleticism and willingness to enter into hostile environments, Gibson created opportunities for African-American athletes for years to come.

One of those for whom the door would open was Arthur Ashe. Unlike Gibson, Ashe was incredibly vocal and insightful about his experiences with racism, bigotry, and injustice. He fought his battles on and off the court, standing up for his own rights and those of others like him. Ashe became the first African-American male to be a member of the US **Davis Cup** team, which represents the country in international tennis competition. He also would become the first African-American male to win at Wimbledon, the Australian Open, and the US Open. Throughout his career, Ashe advocated for the rights of his fellow tennis players by helping to form the **Association of Tennis Professionals**. This union gave the athletes more say in their schedules and more opportunities to increase their share of the sport's growing revenues. He created youth tennis programs to reach disadvantaged children, and he became a staunch and vocal opponent of South Africa's **apartheid** policies, which suppressed blacks in that country. In his later years, Ashe became known for his role as an **ambassador** in **Human Immunodeficiency Virus** (HIV) and **Acquired Immunodeficiency Syndrome** (AIDS) awareness, after he was diagnosed with the disease. Ashe cared much about his success on the tennis court, but he also used it as a platform to further bring light to issues of grave importance.

Althea Gibson earned respect at a young age, when many onlookers couldn't help but take notice of her talent. Here, she collects a trophy in the late 1940s.

CHAPTER 1

COURTING SUCCESS

"If I've made it, it's half because I was game to take a wicked amount of punishment along the way and half because there were an awful lot of people who cared enough to help me."

—Althea Gibson in her autobiography,
I Always Wanted to Be Somebody

Althea Gibson was born in Silver, South Carolina, on August 25, 1927. At age three, Gibson moved with her family to Harlem, New York. She became a regular in the games played on the neighborhood streets, where she was known to spend her time instead of going to school. Gibson would skip weeks of school and then refuse to go home for days to escape the wrath of her father. She even lived in the Society for the Prevention of Cruelty to Children as a homeless teenager until her father agreed not to physically punish her anymore. "My parents were doing their best to raise me, but I wouldn't let them," recalled Gibson in her biography, *Born to Win*. "I just wanted to play, play, play. My mother would send me out with money for bread, and I'd be out from morning to dark—and not bring home the bread. ... I played it all—basketball, shuffleboard, badminton, volleyball. Mama could never get me up from the street."

Even the beatings couldn't keep Gibson's behavior in check. She wanted to compete, which is probably because she always won. With Harlem being overcrowded, the city had blocked off some streets from traffic in order for the children to have recreation areas. Gibson's family lived conveniently in one such closed-off block, which turned out to be the perfect setting for Gibson to develop.

She grew quickly as a child to almost six feet (1.8 meters) tall, and her father, looking to hone her athletic prowess, taught her to box. He thought if she was as drawn to life on the streets as she seemed to be, she might as well be able to defend herself. However, Gibson made it clear early on that she preferred baseball and paddle tennis. The summer after she finished junior high school, she became her neighborhood paddle tennis champion, and then played the champions from other neighborhoods. She beat them, too.

Her performances were dominating, and they began catching the attention of neighborhood onlookers. Musician Buddy Walker, a volunteer "play leader" on Gibson's block, thought she could handle the next level of competition and bought Gibson her first tennis racket. He taught her to practice by hitting a ball off the wall at the playground's handball court. Walker arranged for a friendly rally at the Harlem River Tennis Courts. "After about ten minutes, all the players on the other courts stopped their games to watch her," he later told the *New York Post*. "In about an hour, spectators had lined up

Althea Gibson helped African Americans overcome years of discrimination with her tennis racket rather than her words.

Dr. Robert Walter Johnson received posthumous recognition by the International Tennis Hall of Fame in 2009. His grandson, Lange Johnson, is pictured here accepting the honor.

on both sides of her court. It was wonderful to see this twelve-year-old kid hypnotize so many people with her speed and power strokes the very first time she had ever been on a tennis court."

Gibson had captured the attention of the more affluent African Americans in the tennis community, namely Juan Serrill, a member of the Cosmopolitan Club. During her visit to the club, which was for African Americans only, the members were so impressed by this phenom that they pooled their resources and bought her a membership. It was there that she learned the rules and etiquette of the game and worked under the tutelage of Fred Johnson, the club's one-armed tennis pro. At the Cosmopolitan Club, she also had a chance to watch Alice Marble, one of the best female tennis players in the world, compete in an exhibition match. Marble would become instrumental in the progression of Gibson's career a few years down the road.

Etiquette Lesson

The members of the Cosmopolitan noted Gibson had more difficulty with her behavior off the court. "I really wasn't the tennis type," Gibson said in *Born to Win*. "I kept wanting to fight the other player every time I started to lose a match." Rhoda Smith, a club member who had lost her own daughter, became a maternal force in Gibson's professional life. Smith told the press, "I was the first woman Althea ever played tennis with, and she resented it because I was always trying to improve her ways. I kept saying, 'Don't do this,' and 'Don't do that,' and sooner or later she would holler, 'Mrs. Smith, you're always pickin' on me.' I guess I was, too, but I had to. When a loose ball rolled onto her court she would simply bat it out of the way in any direction at all instead of politely sending it back to the player it belonged to, as is done in tennis. But Althea had played in the street all her life, and she just didn't know any better."

Gibson wrote in her autobiography, *I Always Wanted to Be Somebody*, that she learned as a teenager to balance her decorum with her game. "After a while," she wrote, "I understood that you could walk out on the court like a lady, all dressed up in immaculate white, be polite to everybody, and still play like a tiger and beat the liver and lights out of the ball." Which is exactly what she did.

While training with the Cosmopolitan Club in 1942, Gibson competed in—and won—her first tournament, the New York State Open, an all-black event sanctioned by the **American Tennis Association (ATA)**. She finished in second place at the ATA United States girl's championship later that summer.

World War II led to the cancellation of many sanctioned events in 1943, but Gibson wasted no time resuming her form once the tournaments were back on. She won the girl's division ATA title in 1944 and again in 1945. Around this time, she also befriended Sugar Ray Robinson, the professional boxer who would long be a Gibson supporter.

In 1946, Gibson competed in her first American Tennis Association adult tournament, where she caught the attention of Dr. Robert Walter Johnson and Dr. Hubert Eaton, prominent members of the ATA, the all-black tennis organization formed in 1916 in response to the **United States Lawn Tennis Association (USLTA)**'s ban of African-American members.

The ATA was instrumental in helping both Gibson and Ashe begin their tennis careers and was well established by the time Gibson was growing up. The ATA held its first national championships in August 1917. It continued to hold events at various historically black colleges and universities, which offered ample housing space in addition to their tennis courts; the organizers

Dr. Robert Walter Johnson hosted budding tennis stars in his home in Lynchburg, Virginia (shown here decades later). The tennis court still exists on the property.

knew that large groups of African Americans would not be accommodated at many hotels, especially in the South. The ATA National Championship soon grew into one of the most anticipated social events of the year in the black community, with formal dances and fashion shows also planned during the week of play.

The ATA also was known for representing the top talent in the African-American community. In 1940, the Cosmopolitan hosted the first **interracial** exhibition matches when Don Budge played against reigning ATA champion Jimmie McDaniel. McDaniel and Richard Weir also competed in a **doubles** match against Budge and his partner, Richard Cohen.

In the adult tournament in 1946, Gibson lost in the finals, but Johnson and Eaton thought Gibson had the potential to win a national championship, so they took her under their wing and served as surrogate parents. Gibson moved to North Carolina, where she got her academics in order and finished high school. She lived with the Eaton family throughout the school year and traveled with Johnson, participating in tournaments during the summer.

Dr. Johnson would remain associated with tennis for many years. In 1953, Johnson began mentoring a ten-year-old boy with notable tennis acumen named Arthur Ashe. Ashe had been working under Ronald Charity, then one of the best African-American tennis players in the nation and a part-time coach. Charity recognized that Ashe needed a proper coach to reach his true potential.

Emotional Ups and Downs

Ashe was born on July 10, 1943, in Richmond, Virginia. He reflected in his autobiography, *Arthur Ashe: Off the Court*, about two monumental events at opposite ends of the emotional spectrum that he had already experienced at that young age. In 1947, his father was hired as a special policeman, which required the family to move to a house in the middle of the 18-acre (7.25-hectare) Brook Field Playground, which became Ashe's haven. But three years later, when Ashe was just seven, his mother died suddenly of complications from a surgical procedure. Her death had a profound effect on his once-happy-go-lucky-father, who would raise Ashe and his brother in a high-discipline household as a single parent until he remarried five years later.

Ashe's refuge often was in the park that served as his backyard. He would watch the students from Virginia Union on the tennis courts, paying particular note to the gifted Charity. The older player noticed Ashe watching and began mentoring this young boy who weighed about 50 pounds (22.7 kilograms). His agility, speed, coordination, and will to win set him apart.

Yet even as a boy, Ashe recognized the role racism could play in restricting his opportunities. As Ashe's father was one of the few African Americans on the police force, Ashe was exposed to and associated with many white individuals and families. He noticed, even as a child, "There was something different about being black … I could not even envision God being black because the pictures of Christ on the back of the fans in my grandmother's church showed him as white," he wrote in *Arthur Ashe: Off the Court*.

Ashe was three years old when Jackie Robinson broke the color barrier in baseball, but racial attitudes were slow to change. He often came face to face with discrimination. He went on a trip to Washington, DC, with his baseball coach and found, "We could not go certain places. Even

Jackie Robinson (*right*) broke down color barriers in baseball against the same racial backdrop as Althea Gibson.

where we were not barred, we were not welcome. I grew up aware that I was a Negro, colored, black […] and other less flattering terms."

Ashe was fortunate there were individuals in the black community focused on assuring the success of young African-American tennis players. Primary among them was Dr. Johnson, who would later be inducted into the International Tennis Hall of Fame. Dr. Johnson invited Ashe to his home in Lynchburg, Virginia, for the summer, as he had done with Gibson, to train against other high-level players and have the opportunity to travel to tournaments. There was a tennis court on the lot next to Dr. Johnson's home.

By the time Ashe came along, Johnson had already fought through racial barriers. He was the first African American granted obstetrical (pregnancy and childbirth) privileges by Lynchburg General Hospital. While attending the USLTA Inter-Scholastic Championship and noticing that all of the boys competing were white, Johnson asked the tournament director if any African Americans had ever played in the tournament. He was told "no" before convincing officials to allow two African-American entrants, from an all-black qualifying event, to participate each year. Ashe was one of those who benefited from Johnson's trailblazing efforts.

Southern Discomfort

Ashe was raised in the South and had to travel only from Richmond to Lynchburg for his summers with Johnson.

Gibson had to trek all the way from Harlem, a move she was reluctant to make because of racial conditions in the South in 1946. She said in *Born to Win* that she'd heard "terrible things were done to Negroes just because they were Negroes, and nobody was ever punished for them."

Gibson didn't suffer physically, but she did go through degrading experiences, beginning in the fall she spent with the Eatons in North Carolina. She was forced to sit in the back of buses, was refused service at some restaurants, and was forced to sit in "Colored Only" sections in others. African Americans had their own hospitals, schools, and playgrounds.

They also had their own tennis tournaments. In the summer of 1947, Gibson hit the road with Dr. Johnson. They traveled to nine tournaments, where she played in women's **singles** and mixed doubles, with Dr. Johnson as her partner. She won seventeen times, nine in singles and eight in mixed doubles. Among her victories was the first of her ten straight titles at the ATA Women's National Championships.

Gibson caught the attention of tennis enthusiasts and officials nationally. During the summer of 1948, Dr. Eaton asked if she would like to play at Forest Hills. Gibson thought it was a joke; exclusive Forest Hills was the location of the US National Championships, from which African Americans had always been banned. But Eaton was serious. He and other higher-ups at the ATA thought Gibson had the talent to break the all-white barrier that had long kept African Americans from USLTA competitions. Arthur E. Francis, then the assistant executive secretary of the ATA, said, "We had wanted for years to break down the unwritten barriers to Negro participation in the USLTA-sanctioned tournaments, but we wanted to be sure we could offer a Negro player who would be worthy of such competition."

Progress was slow. Gibson initially was allowed to play in the Eastern Indoor Championships, which were held in Harlem—only blocks from where she grew up. The pushback from the officials at that tournament was limited at the time, as indoor events were held at public facilities, which didn't have the discriminatory policies of the private sector. The outdoor events were the ones held at white-only country clubs, where strict rules existed about who could compete and who could not.

Expanding Horizons

In her first official competition against white athletes, Gibson won her first two matches to advance to the final eight. She lost in the quarterfinal but had performed well enough to earn an invitation to the National Indoor Championships the following week. She again progressed to the quarterfinals, proving she was among the top eight female tennis players in the nation. She noted in her memoir that she enjoyed the warm reception from her fellow competitors: "I was made to feel right at home by the other girls. It wasn't just that they were polite; they were really friendly. And believe me, like any Negro, I'm an expert at telling the difference. It was as though they realized how much of a strain I was under, and they wanted to do whatever they could to help."

The month of June 1949 was monumental for Gibson in a different sense: she graduated from high school at the age of twenty-one. Gibson was eager to reclaim her independence, and she left her home with the Eatons two days after graduation. She spent her summer winning every ATA tournament she competed in while taking two courses and preparing for college. Notably, she was not competing in the outdoor USLTA events. The private, white clubs hadn't budged on their stance.

With her diploma finally in hand, she was offered and accepted a full scholarship to Florida A&M University, one of the country's largest all-black colleges. Tennis scholarships didn't exist at the time, so Gibson was admitted on a basketball scholarship—her athleticism, competitive attitude, and height of 5 feet 11 inches (1.8 meters) made it a natural fit—and ultimately became a star forward on a team that won the conference championship. In addition to the women's tennis team, she also played on the men's golf team.

While the ATA continued the battle for inclusion off the courts, Gibson made her case on them. She returned to the Eastern Indoor Championships in 1950 and made it to the finals this time, where she lost to

Nancy Chaffee. More people took notice, particularly the Florida A&M student body, which greeted her at the train station upon her return to campus. A band played, and the school president gave a speech, but still, the message of success fell on deaf ears.

Race, it was understood, may not have been the only factor at play. Tennis was not just a sport for white people, but a sport for *rich* white people—and Gibson was neither. Many have conjectured that Jackie Robinson had already been accepted on the baseball diamond because baseball was considered more of a game for the common person. Tennis was strictly meant to be for the elite, many thought. While Gibson had certainly sharpened up her skills, she was neither rich nor white.

TIME

THE WEEKLY NEWSMAGAZINE

Althea Gibson was pictured on the cover of *Time* magazine on August 26, 1957.

ALTHEA GIBSON

Althea Gibson and Arthur Ashe: Breaking Down Tennis's Color Barrier

CHAPTER 2

PASSING A TEST

"I would not have had the chance to do what I have been able to do if Althea Gibson had not blazed the way for me."

—Arthur Ashe, in a speech at Northeastern University's Center for the Study of Sport in Society

Unlike Ashe, who positioned himself as a representative of the African-American community, Gibson was reluctant to champion any causes or take the responsibility of integration on her shoulders. Ashe considered ways in which he could chart his course to better the road for those who would follow in his tracks. Gibson had a more specific and focused goal: she wanted to play.

With less interest in creating a public persona outside of her athleticism, Gibson needed backing from powerful people to make her journey to the courts possible. Some of these people ended up being similar to those who had been barricading her from competition, as they were rich and white themselves. One of Gibson's early idols reentered the picture. Alice Marble, whom Gibson had watched play an exhibition match at the Cosmopolitan Club, knew excluding Gibson due to her skin color was wrong. At this time, Marble was a four-time national champion, so her voice was one that others listened to.

Marble later revealed in a letter that a long-time USLTA committee member had shared with her that Gibson would need to perform well at major eastern lawn tournaments in order to be considered for an invitation to compete at Forest Hills. Those other major tournaments also were invitational, and they hadn't extended invitations to Gibson either. In an article for the July 1, 1950 edition of *American Lawn Tennis*, the official publication for the USLTA, Marble wrote:

"If she is not invited to participate in [those tournaments], as my committee member freely predicted, then she obviously will not be able to prove anything at all, and it will be the reluctant duty of the committee to reject her entry at Forest Hills.

"Miss Gibson is over a very cunningly wrought barrel, and I can only hope to loosen a few of its staves with one lone opinion. I think it's time we faced a few facts. If tennis is a game for ladies and gentlemen, it's also time we acted more like gentle people and less like sanctimonious hypocrites.

"She is not being judged by the yardstick of her ability, but by the fact that her pigmentation is somewhat different. She is a fellow tennis player and, as such, deserving of the chance I had to prove myself. I've never met Miss Gibson, but, to me, she is a fellow human being to whom equal privileges ought to be extended.

"If there is anything left in the name of sportsmanship, it's more than time to display what it means to us. If Althea Gibson represents a challenge to the present crop of women players, it's only fair that they should meet that challenge on the courts, where tennis is played. I know those girls, and I can't think of one who would refuse to meet Miss Gibson in competition. She might be soundly beaten for awhile—but she has a much better chance on the courts than in the inner sanctum of the committee, where a different kind of game is being played."

Too Good to Ignore

Gibson's talent would no longer be ignored. She played in the Eastern Grass Court Championships, her first country club tournament, at the Orange Lawn Tennis Club in South Orange, New Jersey. She won her first match but lost in the second round. The next week, she competed in the National Clay Courts Championships in Chicago, Illinois, winning two matches before being eliminated in the third round.

As the summer progressed, Forest Hills loomed ahead on the calendar. On August 16, the *New York Times* reported the receipt of Gibson's application to compete, writing: "The entry of Miss Althea Gibson has been received, the United States Lawn Tennis Association said yesterday, but it will not be known until next week whether the New York Negro girl will be permitted to play in the national championship starting on August 28 at Forest Hills."

Meanwhile, Gibson was competing for her fourth title at the ATA championships in Wilberforce, Ohio, which she would win. On August 21, 1950, a few days before her twenty-third birthday, Gibson heard the news that

Althea Gibson (*left*) ultimately lost to Louise Brough (*right*) in her first experience at the National Tennis Championships.

the USLTA president had determined: "Miss Gibson was accepted on her ability." She remarked in *Born to Win*, "Although the USLTA announced it in matter-of-fact fashion, there was nothing matter-of-fact about it to me."

Lester Rodney, a journalist for *The Daily Worker* who had championed the desegregation of baseball, considered how monumental the moment would be. He wrote of the West Side Tennis Club at Forest Hills: "No Negro player, man or woman, has ever set foot on one of these courts. In many ways, it's even a tougher personal Jim Crow-busting assignment than was Jackie Robinson's when he first stepped out of the Brooklyn Dodgers dugout."

The reception at Forest Hills was mixed. She found the most support from her fellow competitors and her most public supporter, Alice Marble, who told Gibson: "Have courage. Remember, you're just like the rest of us," Gibson recalled in *Born to Win*. Meanwhile, hecklers hurled insults at Gibson, screaming, "Knock her out of there" and worse. Gibson credits her naiveté and unabashed confidence in blocking out the noise. "I was too arrogant and antisocial," she said. "I was not conscious of the racial difference."

Years after baseball, football, and basketball had integrated at the highest levels, Gibson's presence at Forest Hills represented the breakthrough on the courts that would pave the way for Ashe a few years later and, over the decades to come, other great African-American tennis players such as Venus and Serena Williams.

On Day One of integrated tennis, Gibson beat Barbara Knapp, 6–2, 6–2. Her second-round match presented a different challenge. Gibson came out nervous against Louise Brough and dropped the first **set**, 6–1. She rallied to win the second, 6–3, and was leading in the third, 7–6, when lightning let loose. It was brought by a fierce thunderstorm that toppled a stone eagle from a corner of the stadium. The rain ceased as quickly as it had begun, but the puddles on the courts led to a longer delay. During the break, an African-American man and woman, whom Gibson did not know, served as a buffer between Gibson and an intense consortium of media members. A war of words erupted between the media and Gibson's supposed protectors, despite Gibson never having expressed a need for their support. Gibson was left shaken. She didn't sleep that night, and her nerves weren't settled when the match resumed the next morning. Brough won the last three **games** and the match, 6–1, 3–6, 9–7. However, Gibson did win respect from members of the press for her showing. A *New York Herald Tribune* editorial stated: "Althea Gibson did not come through the tournament with a crown of victory, but she won something she can cherish throughout her life, which never can be taken from her—the respect and admiration of all who saw her play at Forest Hills. She is a credit not only to the Negro race but to all good sportsmen and women who play and love the game of tennis."

Showing Gratitude

Gibson experienced an ugly torrent of racism at Forest Hills and also saw hecklers direct their barbs at Alice Marble. Gibson responded with gratitude and apologized to Marble in a six-page letter, some of which was published in the *Baltimore Afro-American* newspaper on January 30, 1951.

Gibson wrote: "Dear Miss Marble, Your open letter in the November issue of *American Lawn Tennis* magazine was read with a mixed feeling of sorrow and elation … I am elated over the opportunity I had to play at Forest Hills, but I am sorry for the slurs you received and the friends you lost. I do believe that you gained more true friends than you lost by writing the very fine article you wrote

Althea Gibson, flanked by supporter Alice Marble, leaves the court at Forest Hills to applause.

in my behalf in the tennis magazine … I am happy that you have no regrets. Again I say I believe the new friends who believe in fair play and democracy will outnumber the few old ones you lost … Next year I hope that I am invited to play in more USLTA tournaments. I don't mind getting beat. The more I am beaten, the more I will learn. Believe me when I say I am sincerely grateful to you for what you have done for me towards making it possible for me to have played at Forest Hills. I do hope to make you proud of your sacrifices … Again I say not a single player participating at my tournament has voiced any objection to playing against a colored player. To the contrary they have been most pleasant, very good sports and seemed to have

SCORECARD

Althea Gibson

Major Titles: Eleven total, five in singles (1957-58 Wimbledon, 1957-58 USLTA, and 1956 French), five in doubles (1956–1958 Wimbledon, 1956 French, 1957 Australian), and one in mixed doubles (1957 USLTA).

ATA Championships: Ten straight in singles (1947–1956), and seven out of eight in mixed doubles (1948–1950 and 1952–1955).

Wightman Cup: Compiled a 5–1 record in 1957–1958.

USLTA Rankings: Ranked in USLTA Top 10 for six years; Finished No.1 in 1957, 1958.

Other Accomplishments: Won US Clay Court singles and doubles titles in 1957; won gold medal in singles in Pan American Games in 1959; World Professional Tennis Champion in 1960.

Awards: Associated Press Woman Athletes of the Year (1957–1958); Florida A&M Athlete of the Century; Florida Sports Hall of Fame; International Tennis Hall of Fame; International Women's Sports Hall of Fame; National Lawn Tennis Hall of Fame; National Women's Hall of Fame; NCAA Theodore Roosevelt Award; *Sports Illustrated* Top 100 Greatest Female Athletes.

SCORECARD

Arthur Ashe

Major Titles: Five total, three in singles (1968, US Open, 1970 Australian Open, 1975 Wimbledon), and two in doubles (1971 French, 1977 Australian).

Davis Cup Record: 28–6 overall, including 27–5 in singles, with titles in 1963, 1968-70, and 1978.

Career Record: 1,141–436 overall, 818–260 in singles and 323–176 in doubles, with 51 titles (33 in singles, 18 in doubles).

USTA Rankings: Finished number two in 1976, a career best.

Other Accomplishments: Won National Interscholastics in 1960; won NCAA singles and doubles titles in 1965; won the US men's hardcourt singles title in 1963 and the US men's clay court singles title in 1967.

Awards: BBC Overseas Sports Personality of the Year (1975); *Sports Illustrated* Sportsman of the Year (1992); Presidential Medal of Freedom (1993); Virginia Sports Hall of Fame; Intercollegiate Tennis Association Hall of Fame; International Tennis Hall of Fame.

Althea Gibson (*right*) receives a congratulatory kiss from Darlene Hard. Gibson beat Hard to become the first African-American woman to win at Wimbledon.

enjoyed their matches, whether won or lost. Then why do some officials object? I do believe that we are going to see many changes next year. I wait with hopeful anticipation for what 1951 might bring."

Indeed, 1951 brought the crumbling of more barriers. Gibson won her first international title, the Caribbean Tennis Championships in Montego Bay, Jamaica. She then became the first African American to compete in a major tournament south of the Mason-Dixon Line. That spring, she flew to Michigan with the financial backing of a committee of Detroiters that included renowned boxer Joe Louis, and she began to train for Wimbledon. Bernard McElwaine, a sportswriter for the *Sunday Pictorial* in the United Kingdom, wrote at the time: "There is one splendid thing about Wimbledon. If a man or woman is good enough, he or she can play—no matter what their creed or color. With the entry of Althea Gibson, a coloured [*sic*] girl from Harlem, another dent has been made in the thick hide of international prejudice. Good luck to her. Her path has not been easy."

Gibson's Wimbledon experience couldn't have been more different from her time spent at Forest Hills, where she had been relegated to a side court, significantly limiting the number of spectators. No, at Wimbledon, Gibson played at Centre Court in front of twenty thousand people. In a back-and-forth battle, Gibson won her first match on those hallowed English grounds, 6–0, 2–6, 6–4. However, she faltered in the second round and was eliminated from the tournament.

In her autobiography, Gibson reflected on Wimbledon and the next several years of her career. "Unfortunately, a pocketful of money wasn't enough to win for me at Wimbledon," she wrote, upon having received financial backing from Joe Louis and a group of African Americans from Detroit. "All I got was more experience. Then it was back to the United States, and a pattern had been set that was to last for a long time. I didn't advance in the game as fast as I had hoped I would, and certainly not as fast as a lot of people thought I should."

The ATA had placed all its bets on Gibson, hoping she would be the one that would lead the white tennis elite to believe that African Americans had a rightful place in their game. No records show ATA members explicitly telling Gibson she *must* win, but it's clear she felt the pressure. She further reflected in her autobiography: "The ATA seemed to have lost interest in me, and I can't say I blamed them much. I kept on winning their tournament every year but I was no bargain in USLTA competition." Gibson was ranked number nine nationally in 1952, number seven in 1953, and number thirteen in 1954.

No Pay to Play

Her tennis future became uncertain, and it wasn't just because of the frustration of her perceived failure. Tennis was not professional during this era, meaning no prize money was awarded, and Gibson had bills to pay. In comparison, Women's Tennis Association events offered $129 million in earnings to participants in 2014. The women ranked in the top fifteen typically earn at least $1 million each year.

Gibson spoke to a journalist for the *Daily Mail* in London about her financial state: "After ten years of it, I am still a poor Negress, as poor as when I was picked off the back streets of Harlem and given the chance to work myself up to stardom. I have traveled to many countries, in Europe, Asia, and Africa, in comfort. I have stayed in the best hotels and met many rich people. I am much richer in knowledge and experience. But I have no money.

"I have no apartment or even a room of my own anywhere in America. I have no clothes beyond those with which I travel around. And I like clothes. Unfortunately, I have no gift for making them, and I can't afford many of the wide variety of cheap, ready-to-wear American dresses which other American girls buy, then throw away after a few months. Mine have to do for a long time.

"I haven't been able to help my mother and my father, and the rest of my family. They are still poor, very poor. My father is a garage hand. My brother and the eldest of my three sisters go out to work. My other two sisters are at home. And my mother can't go out to work because she's too busy keeping house for the family. I am the eldest of the five children, so you can imagine how badly I feel about not helping them when I am living well and meeting all sorts of fine people."

At the time, Gibson was earning an annual salary of $2,800 to work in the physical education department at Lincoln University in Jefferson City, Missouri. After two years of employment and having fallen in love with an army captain, Gibson seriously considered enrolling in the Women's Army Corps. She was intrigued by the steady paycheck, the opportunity to spend more time with the army captain, and maybe one day becoming an officer. She made the argument to Sydney Llewellyn, then her coach, that she would have won already if she ever was meant to. "If I was any good I'd be the champ now," she recalled telling him in her autobiography. "But I'm just not good enough. I'm probably never going to be."

Reluctant Ambassador

Ultimately, though, she reflected on the time she had put into developing her game, as well as the efforts of many of her supporters. A trip offer to Southeast Asia then came at the perfect time. Gibson, along with another woman and two male tennis players, were to be ambassadors for the US State Department on a goodwill tour in 1955. She played tennis, sure, but the liveliness of the trip more than anything else seems to have reinvigorated Gibson. She recalled searching for a beauty salon in foreign countries, being riveted by dancing girls, eating Burmese-style with her hands, and riding trains in India with just enough room for the beds. Gibson was the principal attraction of the group and was often asked to be a spokesperson for the state of race relations in the United States. Unlike Arthur Ashe, who embraced his role as a spokesman for black people and was a vocal proponent of breaking down barriers, Gibson just wanted to be able to play tennis without the deeper meaning everyone placed on her success or failures as an African American.

In her autobiography, she poignantly wrote, "Personally, I could have wished, as I always have in such circumstances, that I might be allowed to play tennis—win or lose—with the same purely individual responsibility assigned to everyone else … I was having enough trouble trying to gain control of my shots and play the best tennis I was capable of playing. Having to contend with crowds hostile to me because of my color, with newspapermen demanding twice as much of me as they did of anybody else simply because my color made me more newsworthy, and even with powerful governments seeking to use me as an instrument of national policy because of my color, seemed to me to be more than anybody should have to bear."

With that mind-set, Gibson remained focused on the courts. She won sixteen of the eighteen tournaments she competed in during that international tour. In 1956, she won the championship of France, later to be named the French Open, becoming the first African American to win any of the world's major singles tennis championships. Wimbledon was up next. Gibson said she was "overtennised" by too much competition in too little time. She was eliminated from the Wimbledon tournament in the quarterfinals. Later that summer, she lost in the finals of the US National Championships.

Gibson had become a household name and would spend the rest of the year participating in the Pacific Southwest

Championships in Los Angeles, the Pan-American in Mexico City, the four most prominent tournaments in Australia, and the championship of Asia in Ceylon. She and good friend Shirley Fry seemed to be splitting the success: Gibson was the champion of Asia, France, and Italy, while Fry was the champion of Wimbledon, the United States, and Australia. As the summer of 1956 came to a close, Gibson reflected in her autobiography: "There was no getting away from it, Shirley had won the big ones and I had won the little ones. It had been very much her year. All the way back to New York, between catnaps, and with the comfortingly steady roar of the four engines in my ears, I thought about what I could do to make 1957 Althea Gibson's year."

Playing to Win

Had Gibson already broken the color barrier? Had she proved that African Americans could participate—and be successful—in the elite white game? Answers to those questions seemed irrelevant to Gibson. She wanted to win, so she set out to do exactly that.

Gibson's primary focus heading into Wimbledon was to go in fresh. Before the tournament even began, Gibson picked out an evening gown for the ball held for the Wimbledon champion and wrote an acceptance speech. Her confidence had peaked; she knew she was the best. Her first match of the tournament ended up being the closest one; she beat Hungary's Suzy Kormoczy, 6–4, 6–4. Prior to the semifinals, she and her opponent, Britain's Christine

Truman, were informed the Duchess of Devonshire was in the royal box and it would be appropriate to curtsy toward her on the way out to the court. In her autobiography, Gibson wrote as much about being worried about curtsying correctly as she did about the 6–1, 6–1 victory that would send her to the finals, which Queen Elizabeth II attended.

The heat was memorable, with temperatures hovering around 100 degrees Fahrenheit (38 degrees Celsius). This caused a record 1,071 fainting spells during the two-week tournament. Instead of being shaken, Gibson said the sweat seemed to loosen her muscles and perfect her aim. After beating American Darlene Hard in the final, 6–3, 6–2, Gibson screamed, "At last! At last!" on her way to a handshake with Hard at the net and congratulations from the queen herself.

At the ball, Gibson gave a lovely speech thanking those who had helped her along the way, including Drs. Johnson and Eaton, her coaches, the ATA and USLTA, and many of her opponents. She then danced with Lew Hoad, a white Australian, who was the Wimbledon men's champion. The fact no one wrote about this dance at the time seems almost an oversight in the historical context.

Less than two months later, nine African-American children tried to enter Central High in Little Rock, Arkansas. The Supreme Court had declared in *Brown v. Board of Education* in 1954 that school **segregation** was unconstitutional, though many states in the Deep South were reluctant to abide by these new federal regulations to integrate the African-American and white students. In

Althea Gibson (*center*) receives the Venus Rosewater Dish that goes to Wimbledon's women's champion on July 6, 1957. Queen Elizabeth II presented the trophy.

the fall of 1957, the Arkansas governor, Orval E. Faubus, sent the Arkansas National Guardsmen to block the high school's door, barring the nine new African-American students from entry and defying the Supreme Court's decision. Faubus later said, "The Supreme Court shut its eyes to all the facts, and in essence said—integration at any price, even if it means the destruction of our school system, our educational processes, and the risk of disorder and violence that could result in the loss of life—perhaps yours … If we are to judge by the results elsewhere, anywhere, once total, or near total integration is effected, the peace, the quiet, the harmony, the pride in our schools, and even the good relations that existed heretofore between the races here, will be gone forever."

A World Away

In a world where politicians with power held such opinions, Gibson danced with a white man, sang "I Can't Give You Anything but Love" as an honorary—and the only African American—member of the All England Club, and played tennis at the highest possible level.

Gibson didn't seem to consider the enormity of her achievements on a racial level until later on. "Shaking hands with the Queen of England was a long way from being forced to sit in the colored section of the bus going into downtown Wilmington, North Carolina," she wrote in her autobiography. "Dancing with the Duke of Devonshire was a long way from not being allowed to bowl

Althea Gibson was honored with a ticker tape parade down Broadway in New York City after her historic win at Wimbledon in 1957.

in Jefferson City, Missouri, because the white customers complained about it."

Gibson would leave Wimbledon with a gold salver, on which were inscribed the names of the Wimbledon champions, and two other mementos that would long be cherished. The first was a letter from Dwight D. Eisenhower, then the president of the United States, who wrote: "Recognizing the odds you faced, we have applauded your courage, persistence and application. Certainly it is not easy for anyone to stand in the center court at Wimbledon and, in the glare of world publicity and under the critical gaze of thousands of spectators, do his or her very best. You met the challenge superbly." The second memento was a newspaper column written in the *New York Post* by Milton Gross, who was with Gibson's parents when the news came over the radio that Gibson was being crowned the Wimbledon champion. He quoted in his column the words of her parents, as Gibson recalled in her autobiography:

"I didn't think she would," my mother said. "I didn't think a Negro girl could go that high."

"I knew she would do it," my father said. "She only wanted to try for the top, and she finally made it. I knew she had the strength to do it."

"Strength?" Milton wanted to know. "What kind of strength do you mean?"

"Physical strength," Daddy said, "and any other kind of strength that's needed."

Gibson was the number one women's tennis player in the world in 1957 and was rewarded with a ticker-tape parade down Broadway in New York City. After winning Wimbledon, she would proceed to win the vaunted US Championships in Forest Hills. Sports journalists voted her the Associated Press Female Athlete of the Year. Her face was on the cover of *Time* magazine, and she became the first African-American woman to appear on the cover of *Sports Illustrated*.

Then, in 1958, she won both again. During one of the celebrations recognizing her achievements, Gibson said: "I never thought I would ever be in such a place, with all my people present, receiving a medal from the mayor of New York just for hitting a little ball around." The medal—and all her trophies—would symbolize more than her on-court accomplishments, of course. She became an example to the African-American youth who continued to face segregation in their schools and discrimination on the streets. She showed the sporting world that African-American talents weren't to be discounted.

Arthur Ashe (*right*) and his doubles partner Hubert Easton competed in the Eastern Junior Tennis Championships in 1959.

CHAPTER 3

OPENING DOORS

"A hustler is someone who doesn't mind working hard to get what he wants out of life, someone who is practical enough to recognize that if something needs to be done, he will figure out a way to do it, even if it may involve some sacrifice."

—Arthur Ashe, in his autobiography, *Off the Court*

If race was an afterthought to Althea Gibson, Arthur Ashe's skin color was one of the first things he noticed about himself. He questioned everything from a young age in Richmond. In 1953, when Eisenhower added the words "under God" to the pledge of allegiance, a ten-year-old Ashe questioned: "Were those words really intended for us?" He knew Yellow Cabs were for whites only, and he had to sit behind the "white line" on the bus. He noticed all the people in control in the city were white men. Ashe categorized the school system as "separate and unequal," as many African-American teachers had only bachelor's degrees and the money spent per pupil was less than on the white students. The curriculum was designed and the training offered to African-American students was simply commensurate with what they could expect to be offered for employment upon graduation.

"A lot of this thinking goes back to my childhood and the unmistakable impression left in black schoolchildren that there is not much they can do beyond being garbagemen or mailmen," Ashe wrote in *Arthur Ashe: Off the Court*. "You might be a policeman, but never a bank president, mayor, or chief of police. Every black kid I knew grew up feeling that certain jobs were off-limits and unattainable, that books and the Pledge of Allegiance said one thing, but once you left school, you had to live in a completely different set of circumstances … The inequities imposed by racism were frustrating, but I was fortunate to be surrounded by a devoted father and other black people determined to push me along, broaden my horizons, and help me develop a sense of myself that ignored the limits white Richmond wanted to impose at the time."

Ashe's path to tennis prominence was an uphill battle, despite Gibson's success. After Jackie Robinson integrated Major League Baseball in 1947, dozens of players from the Negro leagues would join him in playing at the country's top level. But Gibson was more of an anomaly. Ashe reflected in *Off the Court*: "There was no reservoir of black talent waiting to walk in if the door ever opened." Which is not to say the progress Gibson made was lost, but as a young boy, Ashe would have few role models in the tennis world.

A scrawny boy who knew both his limits and his strengths, Ashe benefitted first from the tutelage of Ronald Charity, who tried entering him into tournaments into which he knew he wouldn't be allowed entry. One he could enter was the

ATA National Championships for boys twelve years old and younger, which Ashe won at age ten in 1953. Charity was instrumental in linking Ashe with Dr. Robert Walter Johnson, who became obsessed with furthering the African-American tennis cause. Johnson saw Ashe's potential and took him on as a student, much the same way he did with Gibson.

Also similar to Gibson, Ashe was forced to learn the etiquette of the game—and the variations of it necessary for African Americans. These included calling an opponent's shot in bounds if you weren't sure where it landed, and, if serving the game before the change of ends, picking up the balls and handing them to your opponent during the crossover. Despite his perceptiveness to racial matters, the gravity of these small moves was somewhat lost on Ashe at the time. He would later write in his memoir: "Dr. Johnson knew we were going into territory that was often hostile and he wanted our behavior to be beyond reproach. It would be years before I understood the emotional toll of repressing anger and natural frustration."

Bonding Experience

During this era, however, Ashe also noticed an increase in the camaraderie of the African-American players and teams. As they wouldn't be allowed in many of the restaurants or hotels, the players and coaches took to eating potluck style with one another while sharing living quarters.

Summer became the time of opportunity for Ashe in his early teen years, as it was during those months that

DOCTOR IN THE HOUSE

Dr. Robert Walter Johnson was the founder of the American Tennis Association Junior Development Program for African-American youth, which introduced the game to children who otherwise may never have had the opportunity to excel. During a time when the United States Lawn Tennis Association blocked all non-whites from competition, the ATA became the prime training ground and tournament host for African Americans and even those of lower socioeconomic status.

After recognizing that he could build his legacy more by coaching than by playing, Johnson built a tennis court in his backyard in Lynchburg, Virginia, where he trained and developed promising African-American tennis players, including Althea Gibson and Arthur Ashe. He taught them the intricacies of the game but also about etiquette and sportsmanship. He mentored almost every significant African-American player who emerged before the 1980s, according to his biography, *Whirlwind: The Godfather of Black Tennis*. Doug Smith, who coauthored the biography, recalled: "To young black kids from the South to come to his house and find a tennis court they could play on was just unbelievable."

Johnson was posthumously inducted into the International Tennis Hall of Fame in 2009. His Hall of Fame biography commends him as he "worked tirelessly behind the scenes to provide opportunities for all competitors, and emerged as a towering figure in the game's evolution."

he was free to travel throughout the country in search of worthy opponents of any race. In 1958, Ashe became the first African American to play in the Maryland boys' championships. In 1959, Ashe played in his first US National Championships at Forest Hills. The sixteen-year-old faced the great Rod Laver, who was twenty-one, and was defeated in the first round.

At age seventeen, Ashe cashed in on Johnson's efforts to get African Americans into USLTA tournaments. In November 1960, Ashe won his first USLTA national title—and the first by any African American—at the National Junior Indoors. That year would end with a scholarship offer from J.D. Morgan, the tennis coach at UCLA. The chance to play tennis and attend college out in California after he finished high school allowed Ashe to envision the sport as part of his long-term future.

With all these opportunities on the horizon, Johnson was focused on Ashe in the short-term. Still-segregated Richmond, where Ashe was limited to African-American competition throughout the winter, would not be the best place to harness and develop Ashe's talents, Johnson decided. As Gibson had done, Ashe left home to live with a friend of Johnson's, Richard Hudlin, in St. Louis, Missouri, for his senior year of high school. Ashe then had the opportunity to compete against any available opponents year-round.

Ashe won the National Junior Indoors again in 1961 and was ranked the fifth-best junior player in the country,

Arthur Ashe became the first African American named to the US Davis Cup team at age twenty in 1963.

despite still having been excluded from major tournaments in Virginia and Kentucky. Those tournaments were held at private clubs that did not allow entrance to African Americans. He was selected to be a member of the Junior Davis Cup team that would travel together to tournaments throughout the summer. The Junior Davis Cup is the international team event in junior tennis; Ashe would be the first African American to represent his country on the largest stage for young tennis players. As a member of the Junior Davis Cup team, the doors opened for him to more fully participate in tournaments across the country.

Frank Deford, the famed sportswriter who would become friends with Ashe, met the budding tennis star when he was in college. Deford devoted a chapter of his autobiography, *Over Time*, to Ashe and wrote about their early time together: "Because of his race, he already had a certain amount of fame, always toting an apposition along with his rackets: 'Arthur Ashe comma the first Negro ever to play [fill in the blank] comma …' and so forth. But he was only one of several good young American players … He was, still, at the time we met, more a racial curiosity than a prospective champion."

Ashe felt the gravity of being the first. "Of course," he wrote in *Off the Court*, "there was a great deal of fuss about being the 'first black' Junior Davis Cup player, the 'first black' to get a tennis scholarship to UCLA, the 'first black' to win Charlottesville, etc. Those comments always put me under pressure to justify my accomplishments on racial grounds, as if sports were the cutting edge of our nation's move toward improved race relations. The fact that this kind of accomplishment by a black player got so much attention was an indication that we still had so far to go."

Building a Platform

Indeed, that message would continue to resonate throughout Ashe's college career. A couple of weeks into his freshman year, Ashe was not invited to join the rest of his teammates in Newport Beach for the Balboa Bay Club's weekend tournament. This denial squashed Ashe's hopes that discrimination and opportunity might be different on the West Coast. He and Morgan, his coach, decided not to fight the decision at the time. Morgan encouraged Ashe to wait until he was more established as a tennis player, so as to fight the racial battles on his own terms.

While in college, Ashe also began to confront questions about his role as a visible African American. One friend urged him to maintain his African-American identity, meaning limited association with whites. Another seemed to suggest that Ashe should be spending as much time in the African-American communities, assisting the youth, as preparing to play tennis. Ashe knew tennis was his platform, but he would not lose sight of the message he hoped to extend.

In 1963, Ashe made his first international tennis appearance when he traveled to Britain to play at Wimbledon. Before even leaving the London airport, Ashe was struck by the class system that existed abroad,

Arthur Ashe joined the Army ROTC to help pay for college. He spent his active duty at West Point leading the academy's tennis team and working as a data processor.

as he saw Indian and Pakistani women cleaning the floors and West Indians and Asians sweeping the streets. He was approached by black Britons who shared their experiences with being blocked from immigration, being unable to live where they wanted to, never being promoted, being unrepresented in the government despite living in "black districts," and having no black members of Parliament. "As much as I love London, I developed a sensitivity there that would apply to every large city I visited," Ashe wrote in *Off the Court*. "Wherever I go, I want to know who does what and specifically, what black people do there." Ashe advanced to the third round of Wimbledon, where he lost to the United States' top-ranked player, Chuck McKinley.

After the tournament, the twenty-year-old Ashe was afforded the ultimate opportunity: he was invited to join the US Davis Cup team and to represent his country at the highest possible level. "Even as race relations in America became increasingly stormy, and I started to feel the attraction of more militant approaches to segregation and racism, I nevertheless saw my Davis Cup appointment as the outstanding honor of my life to that point," he wrote in *Days of Grace*. "Since no black American had ever been on the team, I was now a part of history. Despite segregation, I loved the United States." Ashe played in only one Davis Cup **tie** (in Davis Cup, a tie is an elimination round of matches between two countries) that year, against Venezuela at Cherry Hills Country Club in Denver, Colorado. His was a "dead rubber" match, the last in a best-of-five series that had already been decided. However, upon its ending, Ashe was thrilled to hear the umpire announce the match had been won not by Ashe but by the United States. Ashe's tennis career at this level would be synonymous with the country that had many times turned its back on him or left him out because of the color of his skin. He finished 1963 as the sixth-ranked player in the United States and with his face on the cover of *World Tennis* magazine.

Ashe continued to build his case for full inclusion with his on-court performances on the collegiate stage.

In 1965, Ashe won the singles and doubles crowns in the NCAA tournament and led his team to the NCAA title. He jumped to being the third-ranked player in the United States. In 1966 and 1967, he advanced to the finals of the Australian Open tournament, where he was defeated both times by Roy Emerson.

While in school, Ashe was a member of the ROTC, the Army's Reserve Officer Training Corps, which required him to join active military service in exchange for money for tuition. After graduating from UCLA in 1966 with a bachelor's degree in business administration, Ashe joined the US Army. He served for two years and was given time off to compete. He was promoted to first lieutenant prior to his discharge. While his ROTC participation provided Ashe with tuition money, it forced him to maintain his **amateur** status as well. In the late 1960s, tennis was transitioning to a different era, a professional one that included significant prize money for its top players. Ashe wouldn't be able to reap the financial benefits quite yet.

A New Era

Ashe kicked off the 1968 season by winning the United States Amateur Championships against Davis Cup Teammate Bob Lutz. Ashe then would compete in the very first US Open (formerly the US National Championships) against professionals. Ashe trounced his opponents through the early rounds of the best-of-five-sets tournament, sweeping his first three in straight sets, then took down Cliff Drysdale in the quarterfinals and Clark Graebner in the semifinals in four sets apiece. Tom Okker, a native of Amsterdam nicknamed "The Flying Dutchman," awaited in the final. Rain delayed the match from Sunday to Monday, so the stands were only half full. Ashe took a grueling first set, 14–12, but Okker won two of the next three. After two hours of tennis, the match was still undecided. With his father and Dr. Johnson in the stands, and in the best shape of his life after two years in the army, Ashe focused on holding his serve. He stuck to the basics, the voices of current and former coaches ringing through his ears. After two hours and forty minutes of back-and-forth tennis, Ashe had another "first" to add to his legacy.

As Ashe was awarded the inaugural trophy for the US Open, he hugged his father, who was crying tears of joy. The *New York Times* called Ashe's victory "the most notable achievement made in the sport by a Negro male athlete." As he technically was an amateur, Ashe could not accept the $14,000 prize winnings, which were given to the runner-up. Instead, Ashe collected $280 in expenses, at $20 per diem for fourteen days, including two days of practice. (Participating as an amateur, and with the Davis Cup team still alive in international play, Ashe avoided having to serve in the Vietnam War.) Ashe capped that year by helping the US team win the Davis Cup. His tally for 1968 was victory in ten of twenty-two tournaments in which he competed, and a 72–10 win-loss record.

Arthur Ashe became the first African-American male to win the US Open, beating Tom Okker (*left*) in 1968.

His successes were already leading to a larger platform. In March 1968, Ashe made his first public speech on account of race, which he gave at Reverend Jefferson Rogers' Church of the Holy Redeemer, despite public presentations being against army regulations. He spoke about black responsibility to the cause of justice. The army told him not to do it again, but Ashe's political fire had been stoked. That April, Martin Luther King Jr., would be assassinated. Two months later, Senator Bobby

Kennedy, who had been a crusader for the African-American Civil Rights movement, also was shot to death. Following his victory in the US Open, Ashe was the first athlete ever invited on the television news program *Face the Nation*. He spoke freely about the role of African Americans in professional sports and how it related to the building momentum that resulted from the civil rights movement.

His time in the army and travels to Southeast Asia and Japan taught Ashe quickly that discrimination was universal: everyone seemed to look down upon someone else on the merits of race or ethnicity alone. "I was beginning to believe that the entire world was stratified by skin color," Ashe wrote in *Off the Court*. "I had to catalogue the phenomenon and make some sense of it for my own value system. South African apartheid aside, there are many explanations about the dominance of light-skinned people in certain jobs and positions of power. I worry about the possible effect of this phenomenon on children who grow up and believe their chances in life are not going to be as good because of their skin color. My travels convinced me of the importance of role models."

If discrimination and racism were underlying themes that Ashe confronted throughout the first twenty-six years of his life, 1969 would bring them to the forefront. In the summer of 1968, Ashe had engaged in a conversation with South African tennis player Cliff Drysdale about the first South African Open that was due to be played that fall. Drysdale told Ashe, "They'd never let you play … You would need a visa to enter South Africa, and the government would never let you have one," Ashe recalled in *Days of Grace*. At first, Drysdale was right. Ashe applied for a visa in 1969 and was rejected. He was rebuffed again in 1970.

Fighting Apartheid

South Africa was then under apartheid, literally translated to "a state of being apart," which upheld segregation in the country from 1948 until 1994. Under apartheid, non-white South Africans were forced to live in separate areas, use separate facilities, and have limited contact with their white counterparts. A series of laws passed that required non-whites to carry documents to authorize their presence in restricted areas. Non-whites were not allowed to participate in the national government. From 1961 to 1994, more than 3.5 million non-whites were forcibly removed from their homes. Their land was sold at a low price to white farmers while they were left in a state of poverty and hopelessness.

In 1970, Ashe traveled to Africa on a goodwill tour and began to strengthen his sense of responsibility to represent the wrongs of apartheid. He traveled with Frank Deford and told the journalist, "We've never had a black athlete in the United States who can do what I've been given the chances to do."

Visiting South Africa and speaking against apartheid became important causes to Arthur Ashe. Here, he talks to youths in Soweto in 1973.

Ashe continued making public anti-apartheid statements, but it would be years before he would set foot in the country. He led efforts to ban South Africa from the international Davis Cup tournament. In the meantime, his tennis game was ascending. In 1970, Ashe won the Australian Open men's singles title, his second Grand Slam victory. He also was an integral piece of the US Davis Cup team, which won every year from 1968 to 1972. During Ashe's fifteen-year career as a member of the Davis Cup team, he would play in thirty-two singles matches and win twenty-seven of them.

In 1973, Ashe's visa to South Africa was approved. Much fuss was made over whether or not Ashe should accept the invitation to compete in the still-segregated country. One argument against increasing his involvement in South African matters was that racism and discrimination still existed on the home front. Another point of debate centered around the idea that if Ashe competed in the white man's South African tournament he was acting as an "Uncle Tom," or a black man who will do anything to stay in good standing with the white people, even if it wasn't in the best interests of his own race.

Ashe decided to go, knowing that he would be doing more than competing and that he would not allow himself to be a show pony for a South African government wishing to demonstrate its "progress." Ashe set ground rules: he would not play in front of a segregated audience; he wouldn't come as an "honorary white;" and he would be allowed to go wherever he wished and say whatever he wanted during his stay. As the terms were agreed to, Ashe headed abroad with a greater mission than playing good tennis. "The core of my opposition to apartheid was undoubtedly my memory of growing up under segregation in Virginia," Ashe wrote in *Days of Grace*. "The WHITES ONLY signs in Johannesburg shocked me back to the days when I could play tennis in Brook Field park with other blacks or with a visiting white player looking for a good game, but not in the many better-equipped public courts reserved for whites."

On the tennis court he performed well, losing in the finals to Jimmy Connors and winning the doubles alongside Tom Okker. He recalled the glee at seeing his name—a black man's name—on the champion's board in this country.

Following the tournament, Ashe visited Stellenbosch University, one of the elite schools in South Africa. There, an anthropology professor with a PhD told Ashe he was an exception to the black race: "You are not completely black," Ashe recalls being told. "You have some white blood in you." Ashe became engaged in a debate about the merits of integration, which was met with brash words about the rioting that took place in the United States in the country's integration attempts. The Afrikaners (South Africans whose ancestors were Dutch), to Ashe's surprise, supported the peace that came with keeping the races separate despite the limited freedom it allowed to the blacks. Ashe attempted to enlighten this crowd about the violence that can follow oppression.

Deford accompanied Ashe on the trip to the university and recalled this debate leading to the most remarkable moment he witnessed on or off the court in his career as a journalist. The only other black at the gathering was a tennis official and salesman named Conrad Johnson. Among Ashe's final remarks were two questions posed directly to the white professor, referencing Johnson: "Why can you vote and this man can't? Why are you free and this man isn't?" Deford wrote in *Over Time*: "I've never seen another athlete throw a touchdown pass or hit a home run or score a goal that was as impressive as what Arthur Ashe did that afternoon, the underdog, all alone, on the road, at a gracious luncheon under the oak trees."

Causes and Competition

Ashe would continue to balance his role as an ambassador for many a cause with his journey toward being the world's number one tennis player. The road led back to Wimbledon in 1975, when on the morning of the men's singles final, Ashe told one of his closest friends that he had a funny feeling he couldn't lose. Never mind that Ashe was up against Jimmy Connors, who in 1974 had won the Australian, Wimbledon and US Open titles in addition to 96 percent of his singles matches. Ashe was ready for the spotlight.

"One of the persistent comments about me in 1974 was that I was always a bridesmaid," Ashe wrote in *Off the Court*. "I had reached the finals of eleven tournaments

A huge underdog, Arthur Ashe (*right*) beat Jimmy Connors to win the men's singles title at Wimbledon in 1975.

but won only two. Some members of the media said I was spending too much time on the administrative side of tennis or with my business ventures and wasn't single-minded enough to get the job done properly. At the time, I resented the criticism; in hindsight, I must admit the critics were partly right. I was involved in too many things to concentrate on my game."

In response, Ashe began 1975 with a trip to Puerto Rico with friends who happened to be world-class athletes. He returned to tip-top shape, with particular attention to improved footwork and conditioning. In preparation for that final match at Wimbledon, Ashe studied Connors's game. "We broke down Jimmy's game, shot by shot," Ashe wrote in *Off the Court*. "His major weakness was the low **forehand** approach shot. Also he liked pace, and he loved opening up the court hitting cross-court. If you tried to open up the court, he would try to open it wider. I had to go wide on both sides with my serves and keep as many balls as possible down the middle. Keep the ball low. And pray."

Ashe reports being in "fifth gear" to start the match, as he won the first two sets, 6–1, 6–1. Connors fought back, winning the third set, 7–5. Connors jumped out to a 3–0 lead in the fourth set before Ashe reestablished his dominance and closed out the set, and the match, 6–4. As Althea Gibson did, Ashe took this moment to reflect on the path that led him to the upper echelon of athletic competition. "It's a long way from Brook Field to

Wimbledon's Centre Court," he wrote in *Off the Court.* "Wimbledon represents the highest achievement in my craft. I reached the pinnacle of an effort that began with Ron Charity in 1950 on a playground in Richmond."

Ashe would have some success over the next several years, including a doubles win in the Australian Open, but he suffered a left heel injury that necessitated surgery in 1977. He worked his way back to fourteenth in the rankings before facing another obstacle. In 1979, while teaching a tennis clinic in New York, Ashe suffered a heart attack and underwent quadruple-bypass surgery. As the chest pains never fully subsided, he officially retired in April 1980, at age thirty-six. He compiled a career record of 818 wins and 260 losses, and he won 51 titles.

However, Ashe wasn't done fashioning his tennis legacy. In the summer of 1980, he was called upon to captain the US Davis Cup team by the president of the United States Tennis Association. Ashe would have the opportunity to choose, build, and guide the team that would represent his country. He inherited a talent pool full of high-spirited personalities, including John McEnroe, Vitas Gerulaitis, and Peter Fleming.

As the sport had become more professional and prize money much more significant, the luster of the Davis Cup had begun to wane. In 1980, top players still were expected to play for the Davis Cup, knowing they would receive money only for expenses. Notably, many top players chose to compete in tournaments offering

Arthur Ashe often said he felt no greater pride than having the opportunity to represent his country in international tennis competition.

prize money instead of Davis Cup ties. However, in 1981, the year Ashe was poised to begin his captaincy, the Davis Cup would begin awarding prize money. The format was also overhauled. Instead of taking the better part of the year to reach the Challenge Round, against the previous year's winner, the schedule was made more player-friendly and would include only sixteen countries, to keep play competitive.

Ashe juggled personalities, lineups, diplomacy, and psychology in an attempt to keep everyone happy. The US Davis Cup team won the championship in 1981 and 1982, with much credit going to McEnroe. In 1983, however, the Americans would be bounced in the first round—and Ashe also would undergo a double-bypass operation. The surgery left him feeling even weaker than the first one, and he agreed to a **blood transfusion** that ultimately would alter his life. With the early exit from the Davis Cup tournament, Ashe had four months to recover unhindered by tennis responsibilities.

His energy was renewed by the start of Davis Cup qualifiers the following year, and he had the added task of having a talented but confrontational Jimmy Connors on the team. With emotions running high, the Americans lost to Sweden in the finals that year, then faced international criticism on their inappropriate conduct. In response, and in fear of losing sponsors, the United States Tennis Association established a conduct policy that each player had to sign in order to participate. McEnroe refused. So did Connors, who publicly stated he had never been a "team man" and had no further interest in Davis Cup competition. The United States lost to West Germany in the quarterfinals, and later that fall, Ashe lost his role as Davis Cup captain "for a perceived lack of discipline and organization on the team," according to *New York Times* sources. In 1985, Ashe also was inducted into the International Tennis Hall of Fame, an appropriate conclusion to this first phase of his life.

Arthur Ashe gave a tearful press conference on April 18, 1992, in which he announced he had contracted HIV, which developed into AIDS, during a 1983 heart operation.

CHAPTER 4

NEW CAUSES
TO CHAMPION

"I know I could never forgive myself if I elected to live without humane purpose, without trying to help the poor and unfortunate, without recognizing that perhaps the purest joy in life comes with trying to help others."

—Arthur Ashe, *Days of Grace*

O n a late summer morning in 1988, Arthur Ashe could not move his hand. A string of doctor's visits followed quickly, which led to a CAT scan, a spinal tap, a blood test, and finally a brain operation. In that procedure, doctors found the cause of his loss of movement. None of his doctors even wanted to share the results with Ashe: he was HIV-positive, and his condition had progressed to AIDS. The blood transfusion he had received in 1983 after his second heart-bypass operation had infected him with the Human Immunodeficiency Virus.

HIV is a virus that attacks the immune system, like the flu or the common cold. However, HIV does not go away. It attacks and destroys a person's T-cells or CD4 cells, which the body uses to fight infections and disease. Over time, it may destroy so many of a person's CD4 cells that the body can no longer fight infection. At this time, a person develops AIDS, which is the last stage of HIV infection. Once a person's HIV advances to this point, he or she is at risk of contracting opportunistic infections, including an extreme form of pneumonia, meningitis, a cancer known as Kaposi's sarcoma, diarrhea, lymphoma, dementia, and tuberculosis. Infected individuals who progress to AIDS typically survive about three years, according to the US government's AIDS information site. Once a person has developed a dangerous opportunistic illness, life expectancy without treatment drops to one year.

In the mid-1990s, antiretroviral therapy was introduced. It helps slow the spread of HIV in a person's body. For this reason, many fewer people who contract HIV today progress all the way to AIDS than previously. Unfortunately for Ashe, his illness advanced to AIDS before his symptoms were caught and before the science had advanced to provide appropriate treatment.

Ashe's diagnosis came as an initial shock to many, as HIV/AIDS at the time was linked to intravenous drug use or homosexual sex. Ashe and his doctors, knowing he was not involved in either, safely presumed his contraction of the disease came from the blood transfusion. During this time, when blood banks were less regulated and blood was not screened for the virus, approximately thirteen thousand people would contract HIV from blood transfusions.

Ashe became a "professional patient," he recalled, adhering strictly to his medication regimen, which included AZT (azidothymidine), a controversial AIDS therapy at the time, as doctors and researchers had not yet established an optimum dose. By 1992, Ashe was taking approximately thirty pills a day.

For four years, Ashe fought the battle against AIDS in relative privacy. He shared his news with close friends and family, choosing to inform only those in his inner circle. Then, in April 1992, a tennis writer at *USA Today* asked Ashe if he had HIV/AIDS. "I am not one to be plagued by fits or gusts of rage, and I try hard to keep calm and subdued at all times," Ashe wrote in *Days of Grace*. "I was taught to remain calm on the tennis court, no matter what the score or how questionable the call or discourteous my opponent. But the anger was building in me that this newspaper, *any* newspaper or any part of the media, could think that it had a right to tell the world that I had AIDS."

Ashe spoke with the newspaper's editor, initially claiming that the public had no right to know. The editor argued back that as Ashe was a public figure, the diagnosis was news. Understanding the news was bound to come out now that the media had caught wind, Ashe decided to get the message out on his own terms. He spent the next day calling approximately thirty-five family members and friends to whom he wished to give the news directly and prepared a statement to deliver on HBO. It came as a surprise to no one that AIDS advocacy would become a part of his retirement, in addition to the multitude of other causes he supported.

Within four months, the Arthur Ashe Foundation for the Defeat of AIDS began to take shape. Knowing the plight of AIDS was experienced across the globe, Ashe decided at least of half the money his foundation raised would go toward research and treatment outside of the United States. Additionally, he advocated teaching sex education and safe sex, while attempting to clear up myths and misconceptions about the disease. In December 1992, he created the Arthur Ashe Institute for Urban Health in Brooklyn, New York, with the intent to address health conditions that disproportionately affect minorities and to reduce health disparities.

Loss of Privacy

Being forced to go public with his AIDS diagnosis led to a shift in Ashe's advocacy efforts toward the end of his life, but the causes dear to his heart had captured much of his time and attention throughout his retirement. In fact, his devotion to ending South African apartheid may have been a contributing factor to the end of his Davis Cup captaincy. During his final year as captain, Ashe was arrested for protesting outside the South African embassy in Washington, DC, during an anti-apartheid rally. "Although certain exceptions come to mind, the prevailing political ambience of tennis has always been a wealth-oriented conservatism of the kind associated in this country with staunch Republicanism and exclusive country clubs," Ashe wrote in *Days of Grace*. "The idea of apartheid in South Africa undoubtedly is abhorrent to some of these people, but the idea of demonstrating in the streets against it might

Arthur Ashe attended a parade for former South African President Nelson Mandela held in New York in 1990.

be even more abhorrent, in practical terms. I respect many of the values of conservatism and Republicanism, but I hate injustice much more than I love decorum."

Ashe spoke to groups of anti-apartheid college students, supporting their efforts. In 1989, he pleaded with the Association of Tennis Professionals not to include two tournaments in Johannesburg, South Africa, on its list of sanctioned events for the coming year. Then, in 1990, Ashe attended the ticker-tape parade honoring Nelson Mandela, who had been imprisoned in South Africa for twenty-seven years for leading peaceful protests against the white ruling class and for political offenses. Apartheid laws were repealed in 1991, and in 1993, non-whites were allowed to vote. In 1994, Mandela was elected president.

Another important role for Ashe was his seat on the board of directors with Aetna Life and Casualty Company. Originally, he assisted primarily with minority recruitment of employees who had the potential to climb up the managerial ladder. Over time, however, Ashe came to view himself as a voice for the sick, who certainly had many needs to be met by insurance companies. He understood the business of an organization as large as Aetna, but he brought his personal experiences and need for medical support into every meeting of which he was a part.

Ashe established ventures in the area of public service, as well. The Ashe-Bollettieri Cities program was established in response to the deteriorating conditions in American cities, which included violent crime, drug abuse, and juvenile delinquency. (Nick Bollettieri is one of the most renowned tennis instructors in the United States.) The program was intended to teach young people life lessons while using tennis to hold their attention. Publicly, Ashe spoke about the untapped potential of inner-city athletes. "America is on the downslide in international tennis competition," Ashe told the *Los Angeles Times*. "We feel that the inner-city community has been overlooked in the training and recruitment of potential world-class players."

Also in the late 1980s, he formed the Safe Passage Foundation. Ashe learned that only one in four African-American athletes in football and basketball at Division I schools ever graduated from college. He saw this as a catastrophic indicator of the difficulty faced by many African Americans in the transition from youth to adulthood, which may have compounded those same statistics of violence, drug use, and poverty. Tennis became the outlet Ashe used to entice the youth to hear his message, often inviting well-known tennis veterans to play exhibition matches in front of rapt audiences.

"We use tennis to attract the kids, but we make sure that we spend about one-third of our time talking about other, more serious matters," Ashe wrote in *Days of Grace*. "I always try to lift the sights of the youngsters to new heights. Trying to be the next Michael Jordan is fine, I tell them; but why not also aim for the goal of owning the team that employs the next Michael Jordan?"

Professional Path

Althea Gibson's post-amateur tennis life, while less filled with activist activities, should not be overlooked. In 1958, shortly after winning her second Wimbledon title, Gibson retired from amateur tennis to become a "professional," which did not have the meaning then that it does today. "I may be the queen of tennis right now, but I reign over an empty bank account, and I'm not going to fill it by playing amateur tennis, even if I remain champ from now until Judgment Day," she wrote in *Born to Win*.

Turning pro meant Gibson would be eligible to receive money for playing tennis—but that doesn't mean anyone was really handing it out. Professional and well-established tours for women were still fifteen years away, meaning opportunities were limited to promotional events. Her skin color continued to prevent her from opportunities, such as becoming a teaching pro at a club. "To hail my talents in public doesn't cost anything," Gibson wrote in *Born to Win*. "But to hire a Negro—and a Negro woman at that—to teach white club members called for a bigger expenditure of courage than most club owners were willing to make." Gibson also found that endorsement opportunities were few and far between. The most lucrative option turned out to be a world tour with the Harlem Globetrotters, for which she would be paid $100,000 to open for the team or play at halftime across a one hundred-game tour. The travel was grueling, but she found comfort in the camaraderie with the African-American basketball players.

Althea Gibson, who signed a contract with Dunlop in 1963, spent years as a professional golfer following her tennis career.

Althea Gibson's enormous athleticism made it possible for her to transition from one sport to another.

In May 1960, at age thirty-two, the two-time Associated Press Female Athlete of the Year and two-time Wimbledon champ put a down payment on a ten-room single-family house in Queens for her family and visiting friends and moved into a two-and-a-half-room apartment, the first home she could call her own.

The other tennis ventures she tried were a flop, but Gibson felt tied to the sports world. Her tremendous athleticism allowed her to make a decision few would be able to; she took up a different professional sport altogether: golf. Those who knew her intimately weren't surprised. *New York Post* columnist Gene Roswell wrote of Gibson: "No sport seems to be beyond her capability. Althea has the muscle and coordination for basketball and baseball, the speed and finesse for tennis, the touch and delicacy of control for pool and ping-pong, and the cold aplomb for golf." Three years after she officially took up the sport, she became the first African-American member of the Ladies Professional Golf Association in 1963.

Gibson's style of play accentuated the capacity of the female athlete. "People always had a stigma that women couldn't do things aggressively," said Renee Powell, a fellow LPGA member and African American who joined the tour in 1967. "Althea showed that you can be a female and excel. And excel with power and grace."

Without touting her barrier-breaking abilities, Gibson recognized the contribution she made to her race and her gender by competing at a high level and forcing clubs to reconsider their discriminatory policies. Not all the walls would be broken down, of course. At certain tournaments she would have to change her clothes in the car, as she was banned from the clubhouses. Some hotels would not allow her to stay in them. "There were a lot of tournaments that wouldn't accept me," she recalled in *Born to Win*. "I don't know if they thought I was going to eat the grass. All I wanted to do was hit the ball off it." Gibson participated in 171 golf tournaments from 1963 to 1971. Her lifetime earnings were less than $25,000 and her highest ranking was twenty-seventh in 1966; she finished tied for second in the 1970 Len Immke Buick Open.

Helping Underprivileged

Gibson spent her retirement years advocating for education for the underprivileged and for youth. In 1972, she began running Pepsi-Cola's national mobile tennis program. It brought portable nets and equipment to underprivileged areas in Atlanta, Boston, Detroit, Newark, New York City, and Philadelphia.

Gibson also directed women's sports and recreation for the Essex County Parks Commission in New Jersey and provided tennis lessons and clinics at the Valley View Racquet Club in Northvale. She was known to recall her upbringing and ability to learn paddle tennis in the streets. "I'm motivated to try to help develop young people in tennis because of the way I came up," Gibson told the Newark *Star-Ledger* in 1972. "I had help, and now I want to use my talents to help others."

In 1976, she was appointed New Jersey's athletic commissioner, the first woman in the entire country to hold the role. She resigned a year later, citing lack of autonomy and inadequate funding. After unsuccessfully running for the state senate, she served as the manager of the Department of Recreation in East Orange, New Jersey. She also served on the State Athletic Control Board and became the supervisor of the Governor's Council on Physical Fitness and Sports.

Gibson was inducted into the National Lawn Tennis Hall of Fame, the Florida Sports Hall of Fame, the Black Athletes Hall of Fame, and the New Jersey Sports Writers Association Hall of Fame. She also was one of the first six inductees into the International Tennis Hall of Fame. Gibson was the first woman to receive the Theodore Roosevelt Award, the highest honor from the National Collegiate Athletic Association, for embodying competitive excellence and good sportsmanship while providing significant contributions to the expanding opportunities for women and minorities.

Althea Gibson (*center*) watches kids learn to play paddle tennis in a city-sponsored program in Harlem in 1973.

GAME-CHANGING CHRONOLOGY

Althea Gibson

1927: Born in Silver, South Carolina.

1930: Moves with family to Harlem, New York.

1940: Neighbors fund her membership to the Cosmopolitan Club.

1941: Wins the American Tennis Association New York State Championship.

1946: Begins training under Dr. Robert Walter Johnson.

1947: Wins the first of ten straight ATA National Championships.

1949: Becomes first African-American woman to play in USLTA's National Indoor Championships; Graduates from high school.

1950: Receives invitation to compete in the United States National Championships (now the US Open); loses in the second round.

1956: Wins French Open, first African American to win a Grand Slam event.

1957 and **1958**: Wins Wimbledon and US National Championships; named Associated Press Female Athlete of the Year.

1964: Becomes first African American to join the Ladies Professional Golf Association tour.

1972: Takes over Pepsi-Cola's national mobile tennis project.

1976: Appointed New Jersey athletic commissioner, the first woman in the country to hold this role.

2003: Dies at the age of seventy-six.

Arthur Ashe

1943: Born in Richmond, Virginia.

1947: Moves with his family to a house near the 18-acre (7.3 ha) Brooke Field Playground.

1950: Ashe's mother dies; he begins learning tennis from Ron Charity.

1953: Begins training under Dr. Robert Walter Johnson.

1958: Becomes first African American to compete in the Maryland boys' championship.

1960: Moves to St. Louis, Missouri, with Richard Hudlin.

1963: Awarded a tennis scholarship to UCLA; becomes the first African American selected for the US Davis Cup team; plays in his first Wimbledon.

1965: Wins the NCAA singles and doubles titles.

1966: Joins the US Army.

1968: Wins the United States Amateur Championships and the first US Open.

1969: Helps found the National Junior Tennis League.

1969 and **1970**: Denied a visa to South Africa due to apartheid laws.

1970: Wins the Australian Open.

1972: Helps with formation of the Association of Tennis Professionals (ATP).

1973: Has visa approved to visit South Africa; wins doubles match at invitational and speaks against apartheid.

1975: Wins Wimbledon final against Jimmy Connors.

1977: Marries Jeanne Moutoussamy.

1980: Retires from tennis following heel and heart surgeries; begins captaincy of US Davis Cup team.

1983: Undergoes double-bypass heart operation and receives blood transfusion, during which he contracts HIV/AIDS.

1986: Adopts daughter with Jeanne, named Camera.

1988: Diagnosed with HIV/AIDS; publishes a three-volume book titled *Hard Road to Glory: A History of the African-American Athlete.*

1992: Publicly announces his HIV/AIDS diagnosis; begins advocacy and raising awareness about AIDS.

1993: Dies from AIDS-related pneumonia at age forty-nine.

Althea Gibson opened the doors for future African-American tennis players, including US Fed Cup team members Venus Williams (*left*), captain Zina Garrison (*holding flag*), and Serena Williams (*second from right*). The other members are Corina Morariu (*center*) and Lindsay Davenport (*right*).

CHAPTER 5
FOLLOWING LEADERS

"Althea Gibson and Arthur Ashe, the first black players to win Grand Slam titles, made my journey less difficult. Their trailblazing careers gave me something to aim for; their guidance gave me something to cherish."

—Zina Garrison, the first African-American captain of the US Fed Cup team and coach of the 2004 US Olympic Team

Althea Gibson and Arthur Ashe left legacies that suggested skin color should not be a limitation. Their influence reached beyond sports, as their athletic successes provided a springboard to launch their faces—African-American faces—into the public consciousness. Because of their abilities, it would become much harder to ignore the talents and potential of African Americans.

Gibson also can be credited with trailblazing athletic opportunities for women. While she was being derided for her unwillingness to sit still and her desire to play whatever game, with whomever and in whatever venue she could, young girls can play today in an entirely different environment. "It is a change in psychological atmosphere," Gibson wrote in *Born to Win*. "In the past, she was discouraged. In the present, she is encouraged. Today, it is no longer considered unfeminine to be in sports." She encouraged girls to compete against boys to develop a greater sense of equality, stating, "By competing at this early age, she learns not to sit back and be pushed aside by men as inferior, nor that to compete is unladylike. So she develops the desire to succeed that will carry over into her business and professional life."

Gibson fought for greater pay equity between male and female athletes, advocated for competition between amateurs and professionals, and emphasized the need for improved facilities and resources for both athletes and the general public. After the 1972 passage of Title IX, which prohibits gender discrimination in education or any programs receiving federal financial assistance, including sports, Gibson pushed to ensure more opportunities—and scholarships did in fact result from her efforts.

The growth of the African-American tennis game was and still is slow. "Tennis is not an integral part of black lifestyles; until that happens we are forcing the issue—really forcing it," Ashe wrote in *Off the Court* in 1981. "When will it happen? Not for a while, because the facilities, competition, and coaching are not freely available in the black community. If a black kid today wants to become a tennis player, in effect he has to leave the black community. He can't do it there. And not that many black kids are confident enough and self-disciplined enough to survive in a white world at an early age."

No African-American tennis stars would emerge in the twelve years between Gibson's first Grand Slam title in France in 1956 and Ashe's first US Open victory in

CARRYING ON THE EXAMPLE

Venus and Serena Williams have become synonymous with tennis played at the highest level. The doors to their tennis world, however, were partially opened because of the trailblazing efforts made by Althea Gibson and Arthur Ashe. Immediately after winning Wimbledon in 2000, Venus reflected on how happy she was that Gibson was alive to witness her victory. Venus wrote the Afterword for Gibson's biography, *Born to Win*, and reflected on the ways in which Gibson and Ashe eased her and her sister's journey to tennis stardom.

Serena Williams (*left*) and sister Venus speak often of their reverence for Althea Gibson.

Venus Williams said she thought of them during her victory at Wimbledon. "Several times during that tournament, I thought about Althea and the difficulties that she faced back in the fifties," Williams wrote. "It had to be hard because people were unable to see past color. At times, they still aren't. I also thought of Arthur Ashe, who won Wimbledon in 1975 and remains the only black man to do so."

Given the accomplishments and legacies left by those who came before her, Williams also reflected on her responsibility to continue sharing their message.

"Like Althea, I, too, feel a need to be a role model," Williams wrote. "We all need to do more to expose people of all backgrounds to our sport. Althea's accomplishments set the stage for my success, but she also made a difference for people of all backgrounds in all areas. Through beneficiaries like me, Serena and many others to come, her legacy will live on."

It may have taken some time, but at least on the women's tennis front, change appears to be approaching. As of August 2014, nine of the top fourteen ranked American women were African American, Asian, Latina, or mixed race.

1968. Ashe won his final Grand Slam at Wimbledon in 1975. The next black man to take center stage would be Frenchman Yannick Noah (the father of basketball player Joakim Noah), who won the French Open in 1983. The dominance of the Williams sisters began with Serena's 1999 US Open victory, which was followed by Venus's victories at the US Open and Wimbledon in 2000 and 2001. Forty-one years passed between Gibson's last title and the Williams sisters' first. Both Williams sisters have publicly acknowledged that their journey would have been much more arduous without Gibson and Ashe's courage and success.

William C. Rhoden, now a sports columnist for the *New York Times*, wrote that Althea Gibson and track star Wilma Rudolph are "without question, the most significant athletic forces among black women in sports history … Even to those blacks who hadn't the slightest idea of where or what Wimbledon was, her victory, like Jackie Robinson's in baseball and Jack Johnson's in boxing, proved again that blacks, when given an opportunity, could compete at any level in American society."

Gibson allowed her actions to speak louder than her words. She said she never dwelled on racism because she wanted to keep her focus on winning on the courts and links, where she could make her strongest contributions. "I wasn't fighting any cause," she said in *Born to Win*. "I was out there trying to do a good job for myself and if it was worthy enough to be good for my people, beautiful."

A statue of Althea Gibson was erected in Branch Brook Park in Newark, New Jersey. Gibson spent her later years in that state.

Gibson died in September 2003, having lived a fairly private life through her final years. Alan Schwartz, the president of the United States Tennis Association, spoke at her funeral and told those who gathered there, "She simply changed the landscape of tennis. Gibson was no less a trailblazer than baseball great Jackie Robinson or tennis champion Arthur Ashe, although she received less recognition for her accomplishments. Arthur Ashe's job was not easy; but if he had to climb a hill, Althea Gibson had to climb a mountain. She was the original breakthrough person."

Ashe fought his battles on the courts and in the public domain. And, like Gibson, much of his focus was on providing opportunities to the next generation. Early in his professional career, in 1969, Ashe, along with Charlie Pasarell and Sheridan Snyder, founded the National Junior Tennis League. The NJTL is designed to provide tennis opportunities to economically disadvantaged children. Today, more than 325,000 under-resourced youth, through more than 600 chapters, are having the opportunity to participate in low-cost or free tennis programs or education. The NJTL was the first organized tennis program in which Venus and Serena Williams participated.

Ashe's legacy has lived on through events carrying his name, such as Arthur Ashe Kids' Day, a grassroots tennis and entertainment event held at Forest Hills the Saturday before the US Open. Families are invited to participate in tennis activities and entertainment events with big-name stars for free. Proceeds from the event help fund the NJTL, now named the National Junior Tennis and Learning Network.

Throughout his career, Ashe also looked out for the interests of his peers. In the early 1970s, when Ashe was one of the most famous athletes in a sport with booming popularity, tennis players were not being financially rewarded despite the increased interest. Ashe, along with Jack Kramer and other professionals, partnered in 1972 to create the Association of Tennis Professionals, which represented the interests of male tennis professionals. Before the ATP was created, players had significantly less control over their earnings or their tournament schedule. In 1974, Ashe was elected president of the ATP and until his death he was a spokesman for his colleagues and their rights. Today, the ATP serves as the governing body of the men's professional tennis circuits; the ATP World tour hosts sixty-two tournaments in thirty-one countries.

More Than an Athlete

Ashe also cared to honor and memorialize the legacy of all African-American athletes. In the 1980s, he taught an honors seminar on "The Black Athlete in Contemporary Society" at Florida Memorial University, a historically black school in Miami. As he prepared his syllabus, Ashe found virtually nothing had been written about the history of African-American involvement in sports in America. Ashe decided to take on the role of rectifying this, and he did so in a three-volume series named *A Hard Road to Glory:*

Arthur Ashe's legacy has been carried on in a number of events, including Arthur Ashe Kids' Day, which is held annually before the US Open.

A History of the African-American Athlete, covering the subject from 1619 to 1985. Ashe recalled this project as an emotional experience. "It dealt so intimately, at almost every stage, with both the triumph and tragedy, the elation and suffering, of blacks as they met not only the physical challenges of their sport but also the gratuitous challenges of racism," he wrote in *Days of Grace*. "No sport was exempt from this painful double history, so that compiling the record was a fairly relentless exposure to disappointment." Famously, Nelson Mandela informed Ashe that he read the series while imprisoned.

Ashe's battle against AIDS would take his life. He succumbed to the disease in 1993 at the age of forty-nine. Many awards were bestowed upon him posthumously, in recognition of his contributions to society. Perhaps the most distinguished was the Presidential Medal of Freedom, the highest honor awarded to civilians in the United States. In presenting the award to Ashe's widow, Jeanne Moutoussamy Ashe, in 1993, President Bill Clinton noted Ashe's ability to battle "his way to the top rung of international tennis—and he did it with an inner strength and outward dignity that marked his game every bit as much as that dazzling crosscourt backhand." Clinton called him "an extraordinary man who lived by the words, 'Thou shalt not close a door behind you.'"

Ashe's widow spoke proudly of her husband's legacy. "It's really important that not just today's generation but generations to come understand him as more than just an athlete, as more than just a patient, as more than just a student and a coach," Moutoussamy Ashe told CNN after his death. "That they'll understand the importance of being a well-rounded human being, that you might not be a great champion, but if you're a well-rounded human being then you can do just about anything to succeed in life."

Ashe's name has come to grace several awards since his passing, including the Arthur Ashe Humanitarian award, which is awarded yearly to a male professional tennis player who demonstrates a commitment to social or humanitarian concerns off the court. Additionally, in its annual awards show, the ESPYs, ESPN has given the Arthur Ashe Courage Award to a person in the sports world who has exhibited courage in the face of adversity. The main stadium of the US Open, which is the largest tennis-specific stadium in the world, has been named Arthur Ashe Stadium.

GLOSSARY

amateur An athlete who has never competed for a monetary prize.

ambassador A representative or messenger of an organization or a country.

American Tennis Association The oldest African-American sports organization in the United States; it was created in 1916.

apartheid A former policy of segregating and oppressing the non-white population in South Africa.

Association of Tennis Professionals The organization created in 1972 to protect the interests of male tennis players.

blood transfusion The direct transferring of blood of one person into the veins of another, done for medical reasons.

civil rights movement Activities whose goals were to end segregation and racial discrimination against African Americans in the United States, starting in the mid-1950s.

Davis Cup The premier international team event in men's tennis, held annually, with each tie consisting of four singles and one doubles match.

doubles A tennis match with four players, two on each side of the court, with wider boundaries than those used for singles.

forehand A tennis swing in which the player hits the ball with his or her palm facing forward; for a right-handed player, a forehand is hit when the ball is to the player's right.

game A sequence of points played with the same player serving; at least four points must be won to capture a game and the winning margin must always be at least two points. It is a segment of a *set.*

Human Immunodeficiency Virus (HIV) A virus that weakens the immune system and can lead to the development of AIDS.

interracial Involving members of different racial groups.

paddle tennis A game similar to tennis, played on smaller courts with a lower net and solid paddles instead of rackets.

segregation The institutional separation of an ethnic, racial, religious, or other minority group from the dominant majority.

set A sequence of games in which players or doubles teams alternate serves; the first player or team to win six games with at least a two-game advantage wins the set. Most tournaments are best-of-three sets, but major or Grand Slam tournaments are best-of-five sets for men.

singles A tennis match played with two players, one on each side of the court.

United States Lawn Tennis Association The precursor to the United States Tennis Association, which originally barred African Americans from participation.

SELECTED BIBLIOGRAPHY

Books

Ashe, Arthur, and Arnold Rampersad. *Days of Grace.* New York: Ballantine Books, 1994.

Gibson, Althea. *I Always Wanted to Be Somebody.* Edited by Ed Fitzgerald. New York: HarperCollins, 1958.

Wimmer, Dick, Ed. *The Women's Game: Great Champions in Women's Sports.* Ithaca, NY: Burford Books, 2000.

Online Articles

American Public Media. "Frank Deford and Arthur Ashe." Interview on NPR's Morning Edition. June 5, 2012. www.thestory.org/stories/2012-06/frank-deford-and-arthur-ashe.

Anderson, Dave. "Ashe Beats Okker to Win Tennis Open." *New York Times.* September 10, 1968. partners.nytimes.com/library/sports/091068ashe.html.

Gittings, Paul. "Arthur Ashe: U.S. Sport's Greatest Black Icon?" *CNN.* September 19, 2013. edition.cnn.com/2013/09/19/sport/tennis/arthur-ashe-james-blake-tennis.

Johnson, Derrel. "Venus Williams Talks Retirement, Fashion, Althea Gibson, and Her Parents." *Rollingout.com.* August 27, 2014. rollingout.com/sports/venus-williams-talks-retirement-fashion-althea-gibson-parents.

McClean, Tony. "A Look Back at 'Whirlwind': The Godfather of Black Tennis." *Black Athlete.* November 11, 2004. blackathlete.net/2004/11/a-look-back-at-whirlwind-the-godfather-of-black-tennis.

Rhodden, William C. "An Emotional Ashe Says That He Has AIDS." *New York Times.* April 9, 1992. www.nytimes.com/1992/04/09/sports/an-emotional-ashe-says-that-he-has-aids.html.

FURTHER INFORMATION

Books

Benson, Michael. *Althea Gibson: Tennis Player*. New York: Ferguson Publishing Company, 2005.

Deford, Frank. *Over Time: My Life as a Sportswriter*. New York: Grove Press, 2013.

Gray, Frances Clayton, and Yanick Rice Lamb. *Born to Win: The Authorized Biography of Althea Gibson*. Hoboken, NJ: Wiley, 2004.

Videos

Arthur Ashe Learning Center Video Guide
www.arthurashe.org/video-archives.html
Those who knew Arthur Ashe best offer their thoughts on the tennis star, plus there are videos of some of the biggest moments from his career.

Game Enough: A Tribute to Althea Gibson
www.youtube.com/watch?v=OBYe7l_msS8
A biography of Althea Gibson in the historical context, with comments from Billie Jean King, Leslie Allen, Bill Cosby, Mayor David Dinkins, and Dr. Harold Freeman.

Wimbledon Men's Final 1975

www.youtube.com/watch?v=GJ2s89U9jKY

Watch the highlights and the trophy presentation from
Arthur Ashe's 1975 Wimbledon victory over Jimmy Connors.

Wimbledon Women's Final 1957

www.youtube.com/watch?v=Bk43frppRHA

Footage of Althea Gibson's 1957 Wimbledon victory, the
first major victory by an African American, male or female.

Organizations

American Tennis Association

www.americantennisassociation.org

The Arthur Ashe Learning Center

www.ArthurAshe.org

ATP World Tour

www.atpworldtour.com

United States Tennis Association

www.usta.com/About-USTA/Organization/History/USTA_
history_archive

INDEX

Page numbers in **boldface** are illustrations. Entries in **boldface** are glossary terms.

Jackie F. Stanmyre is a former award-winning journalist at the *Star-Ledger* of Newark, New Jersey, where she wrote enterprise stories on issues surrounding athletics in addition to extensive profiles about interesting personalities in sports. She currently works as a mental health and addiction counselor. She lives in Montclair, New Jersey, with her husband, son, and their two cats.